Why I am Still
a Christian

Why I am Still a Christian

Hans Küng

continuum

Continuum International Publishing Group
The Tower Building   15 East 26th Street
11 York Road   New York, NY 10010
London
SE1 7NX

Authorized English Translation of *Woran man sich
Halten kann* © T&T Clark, 1987.
English translation edited by E. C. Hughes

Originally published in German in the series
Theologische Meditationen © Benziger Verlag, Zurich/Einsiedeln/Cologne, 1985

First printed 1987
Reprinted 1992, 2001
This impression 2005

British Library Cataloguing-in-Publication Data
A catalogue record for this book is available from the British Library.

ISBN: 0826476988 (paperback)

Library of Congress Cataloguing-in-Publication Data
A catalog record for this book is available from the library of Congress.

Printed and bound in Great Britain by MPG Books Ltd, Cornwall

To the Institute for Ecumenical Research of the
University of Tübingen for its 20th anniversary

Contents

Preface

At a time when great changes are taking place in the Church and society, theologians must reflect deeply and critically. Some of my own thinking has been published in books such as *On Being a Christian, Does God Exist?* and *Eternal Life?* But I am only too conscious how dauntingly large these books are and that most people are far too busy in their hard-working lives to read them through, or put off by difficult scholarly language. I am equally aware that such busy people are just as concerned about the present situation in the Church and society and that they too are anxious to know what uncertain Christians can really rely on these days, and in the days to come.

In this little book I have therefore tried to set out as simply and briefly as possible much of what I have written about at greater length elsewhere on the importance of Christian commitment, and I hope that many readers who would not otherwise venture to read a serious work of theology (and also many that would) will find it helpful.

Tübingen, October 1986   Hans Küng

CHRISTIAN COMMITMENT IN A DISORIENTATED SOCIETY

1.

Disorientation and Christian Commitment

What can we still rely on today? What can we hold on to? I am not a pessimist, but we scarcely need reminding that we are now in a 'crisis' of values as profound as it is far-reaching. Ever since the youth and student revolts of the late 1960s, there are no longer any institutions or guardians of values which are not in crisis or have not been radically challenged. Where today is there any undisputed authority? We used to be told: the pope, the bishop, the church says; or the prime minister, the government, the party says; or the teacher, the professor, 'your father' says. Where nowadays could we even settle a discussion—let alone pacify a demonstration—with an appeal to such authorities? No; the state, church, courts, army, school, family—all seem to be insecure. They are no longer accepted without question—least of all by young people—as guardians of values.

With this critical questioning of accepted authorities, traditions and ways of life, the values associated with them seem to be called into question as well. Liberalisation was necessary, but often went further than had been foreseen or planned. Elaborate processes designed to get rid of taboos frequently turned out to be more destructive than creative, with the result that for many people today, morality as a whole seems to have become relative. The effects of all these developments have been anything but liberating. The ground has been cut from under the feet of some people—especially the young—who now feel their lives have no meaning and turn to delinquency, or extreme religious sects, or to political fanaticism, even terrorism.

This large-scale crisis of values has thrown modern society into conflicts which have not yet by any means been resolved. Indeed their full significance has probably not even been grasped. For our grandfathers and grandmothers, religion, or Christianity, was still a matter of personal conviction. For our fathers and mothers it was still at least a matter of tradition and 'the done thing'. For their emancipated sons and daughters, however, it is becoming increasingly a thing of the past which is no longer binding; passed by and obsolete. And there are parents today who observe with perplexity that morality in general has also vanished, along with religion, as Nietzsche predicted. For—as is becoming increasingly clear—it is not so easy to justify any moral values purely rationally, by reason alone, as Sigmund

Freud would have liked to do; to prove by reason alone why under any circumstances freedom is supposed to be better than oppression, justice better than self-interest, non-violence better than violence, love better than hate, peace better than war. Or, to put it more forcefully: why, if it is to our advantage and our personal happiness, should we not just as well lie, steal, commit adultery and murder; indeed, why should we be humane or even 'fair'?

Perhaps what is good is simply whatever is to my advantage, to the advantage of my group, party, class, race, or even to the advantage of my business or trade union? Is it not a question of individual or collective selfishness? Some biologists and ethnologists do in fact try to persuade us that for human beings, as for animals, any sort of altruism or love is merely the supreme form of biologically inherited self-interest. And, after all, philosophers have continually asked where we are to find the criteria to judge the interests lying behind all knowledge—how we are to distinguish between what is true and what is illusory, what is objective and what is subjective, what is acceptable and what is reprehensible.

So the question remains: how are we to lay down priorities and preferences on a purely rational basis? Purely philosophical arguments to establish essential values have not come up with anything conclusive. They have never got beyond problematical generalisations, which all tend to break down precisely in those exceptional circumstances where people do act in a way that is by no means to their own advantage or for their own personal happiness, but in a way which may involve a sacrifice: even, in an extreme case, the sacrifice of life itself.

How do we know today what we can still rely on, in the last resort? Certainly every day we receive more and more rules of behaviour, 'traffic regulations', maxims. But as we all know, regimentation is not the same thing as having values. On the contrary, the more regulations, regimentation, planning and organisation we have, and the more that laws, requirements, forms and 'the pressure of circumstances' gain control in all spheres of life, the more people feel disorientated and lose insight and oversight; and the more people feel to be losing control over their lives, the more they demand clear signposts to help them through the confusion of rules, regulations and outside pressures. In this disorientated age people long for a fundamental orientation, for some system of essential values, for a commitment. It is the commitment to these *essential* values, not to society's superficial rules and regulations, which is the theme of this book.

As I said, I am not a pessimist. People are no worse today than they were in the past, when values were more abundant. Young people have always been 'bad', according to their elders. But this much must be said, if we are to understand the present younger generation in particular; social change has never come about with such speed and complexity as it does today. Consequently, it becomes increasingly difficult to hold on to essential values, and the danger of spiritual homelessness and rootlessness is growing all the time. Everyone—young and old—is trying to work things out for themselves, often quite naïvely. Some people orientate their lives by the horoscope, others—more scientifically minded—by biological rhythms; some organise everything according to a planned diet, others according to yoga; one person swears by group therapy, another by transcendental meditation, a third by political action. But it is not merely a question of individual values; it is a matter of social values as well. Ethical questions abound: nuclear energy, gene manipulation, test-tube babies, environmental protection, East-West and North-South conflicts; and it is becoming increasingly clear that such questions are exceeding the comprehension and overtaxing the powers of individuals. Today we can do more than ever—but what we *should* do we simply do not know.

It is obvious that I cannot address all these complicated questions in this brief reflection. But perhaps I can say something of fundamental importance towards their solution, something which our educational system, geared as it is primarily towards the acquisition of knowledge and diplomas, ought to pay more attention. Perhaps I can say something that will help provide some ground under our feet, a vantage point, from which all individual problems may be judged: the basis for a commitment to the essential values, that is to say the essential *Christian values*.

But it is at this very point that inhibitions arise. So, after this first section on the crisis of values, let me in the second section make a few comments which will lead us in the right direction. In this context I should like to introduce the important distinction between what is 'nominally Christian' and what is 'truly Christian'.

2.

The Nominally Christian and the Truly Christian

Here I should like to speak not only to Christians but to non-Christians also, as well as to the many people who simply doubt. Perhaps Christians and non-Christians alike can agree initially on three important points:

○ In the present crisis of values, most people are convinced that without the minimum degree of consensus about systems of values it is impossible for human beings to live together at all. Without the minimum degree of consensus about received, basic norms and attitudes (and these things are certainly under serious discussion in the different political parties today), it is questionable whether even the state can function, in view of all the conflicting interests. We can assume that there is agreement about one point at least—that there can be no civilised society and no state without some system of laws. But no legal system can exist without a sense of justice. And no sense of

9

justice can exist without a moral sense or ethic. And there can be no moral sense or ethic without basic norms, attitudes and values.

○ If (as I have suggested) it is exceedingly difficult, if not impossible, to justify ethics purely rationally, then we cannot recklessly ignore the significance and function of the phenomenon which for thousands of years has offered the justification for an ethic and for the basic values of men and women. That is to say, we cannot put religion aside without accepting the consequences. We must accept that there is no unconditionally binding obligation to perform a particular humane action without the acceptance of an unconditionally binding authority which lays that obligation upon us. There is no unconditionally binding moral, humane action and no unconditionally binding ethic without religion. And if it is not true religion which performs this function, it will be pseudo-religion or quasi-religion. But for true religion, the sole authority which is permitted to claim absolute, unconditional obedience is nothing humanly conditioned at all; it is the Absolute itself, to which we give the name of God.

○ Whether or not we are Christians, we have to admit that the purely humane, basic norms and values of the past were always Christian in character. And this was entirely for the benefit of human happiness and well-being. It was the Christian mind and spirit that enshrined the values of human dignity, liberty, justice, solidarity and peace. Without the Christian content, they would be, and are, equivocal concepts, manipulated at will in both East and West. (It is not only the Peoples' Republics and George Orwell's *1984* which make that plain.) Moreover, whether we like it or not, the Christian message does not offer merely a theoretical and abstract answer to questions about basic norms and values. It is a practical and concrete answer.

The future belongs to the young and so it is they in particular who must face this urgent question: ought we not to take more seriously again the familiar system of values which can help us determine what to do? I am not suggesting a nostalgic retreat into the past; but perhaps we should chart our future course with the help of a certain ancient compass, which may not have outlived its usefulness after all? A compass which—after many other instruments have proved to have given only unreliable bearings in the tempests of modern times—could perhaps point us a course towards a future of greater human dignity? A compass that might reorientate us with essential Christian values once more, and in a new way, in an era whose values have been so impoverished. But here we have to make some distinctions.

For now I can already hear the protests of the non-Christians. Essential Christian values! What is Christian supposed to mean today? Christianity is finished. But here I should like to explain myself to these people too, the non-Christians, the unbelievers. Not only the unbelievers outside but the unbeliever within, in ourselves, who repeatedly raises doubts and objections, who says 'I believe' but, like the man in the Gospel, adds: 'Help my unbelief!' To these people I should like to give a frank and honest answer.

Frankly and honestly: if many people, whether they consider themselves believers or unbelievers, in considering the possibility of essential Christian values, reject everything that has to do in any way with an authoritarian, unintelligible dogmatics or an unrealistic, narrow-minded morality, then I cannot contradict them. If they are exasperated with the legalism and opportunism, arrogance and intolerance of so many ecclesiastical functionaries and theologians; if they want to attack the superficial piety of the pious, the boring mediocrity of many church newspapers and magazines, and the absence of creative people in the church, I am on their side. Nor am I by any means ignorant of the failure of Christianity in history. For I have no intention of whitewashing the history of Christianity, or glossing over its defects: not only the persecutions of our Jewish brothers and sisters, the crusades, the heretic trials, the witch burnings and the religious wars; but also the Galileo trial and the countless wrong condemnations of ideas and people—scientists, philosophers and theologians; and all the involvements of the church in particular systems of society, government and thought; and all its many failures in the slavery question, the war question, the women's question, the class question and the race question; and the manifold complicity of the churches with the rulers of various countries in their neglect of the despised, downtrodden, oppressed and exploited peoples; and religion as the opium of the people .... Everywhere here criticism, severe criticism, is appropriate.

But I ask you: is all this even 'Christian'? Believers and unbelievers must affirm that it is 'Christian' only in a traditional, superficial and untrue sense. Christendom certainly cannot shed its responsibility for what is *called* 'Christian'. But none of this is Christian in the deeper, pure, original sense; none of it is truly Christian. It has nothing to do with the Christ to whose name it appeals. In many ways it is part of what brought him to the cross. It is in fact pseudo-Christian or anti-Christian.

There is so much that is *called* Christian. But is it all Christian just because it is called Christian? We must face up to this question. Even people who acknowledge that they belong to a Christian church—as I do, with complete conviction—would not wish to maintain that everything connected with institutional upholders of Christianity is Christian.

No, with the best will in the world I cannot call it Christian, or possessed of genuine Christian values, when in my own church for example ecclesiastical authority alone is involved, instead of Jesus Christ himself, in questions which are important for millions of Catholics. I must repeat: with the best will in the world, I cannot think that the One to whom Christianity appeals, Jesus of Nazareth himself, would today take up the same attitude as the Roman authorities in the questions at issue. I cannot believe

○ that he, who warned the Pharisees against laying intolerable burdens on people's shoulders would today declare all 'artificial' contraception to be mortal sin;

○ that he, who particularly invited failures to his table, would forbid all remarried divorced people ever to approach that table;

○ that he, who was constantly accompanied by women (who provided for his keep), and whose apostles, except for Paul, were all married and remained so, would today have forbidden marriage to all ordained men, and ordination to all women;

○ that he, who said 'I have compassion on the crowd', would have increasingly deprived congregations of their pastors and allowed a system of pastoral care built up over a period of a thousand years to collapse;

○ that he, who defended the adulteress and sinners, would pass such harsh verdicts in delicate questions requiring discriminating and critical judgment, like pre-marital sex, homosexuality and abortion.

No, I cannot think either that, if he came again today, he would agree

○ that difference of denomination should continue to be considered an impediment to marriage—indeed that such a marriage should recently have been made an obstacle for Catholic lay theologians who wish to engage in pastoral service (as is also true for Protestant would-be pastors);

○ that the validity of the ordination of Protestant pastors and their eucharistic celebration should be disputed; that open communion and common celebration of the Eucharist, shared church buildings and parish centres and ecumenical religious instruction should be prevented; indeed that ecumenical services should be systematically forbidden on Sundays, in an era of increasingly empty churches;

○ that, instead of entering into open and

reasonable debate, the attempt should be made to silence theologians, university chaplains, teachers of religion, journalists, organisational officers and people responsible for youth work with decrees and 'declarations' (and even, whenever possible, with disciplinary or financial measures).

No, if we want to be Christian, we cannot demand freedom and human rights for the church externally and not grant them internally. We cannot replace urgently needed reforms in the church by fine words about Europe, the Third World and the North-South conflict at synods, church assemblies and papal rallies. To put it briefly, justice and freedom cannot be preached only where it costs the church and its leaders nothing.

I could easily go on and talk, for example, about the use of public money without official controls; or about financial scandals in Rome, Chicago and other places. I could mention the nomination of bishops, contrary to ancient Catholic tradition, without the participation of clergy and people, or of priests and diocesan councils; or the continual disregard paid to the age limit of 75 for bishops, a principle solemnly laid down by Vatican II; and so on.

I mention all this so openly, not because it gives me any pleasure to do so, but simply because it is the theologian's duty and responsibility to speak the truth, whether it is opportune or inopportune, even if punishment might follow.

But, although I am aware of the sinister nature of much of what is *called* Christian, and although I am aware also of the most important scientific, scholarly or popular objections to Christianity—historical, philosophical, psychological or socio-logical—I should nonetheless like to say this: that in this disorientated age I receive my essential values from Christianity, despite everything. Not from what is *called* Christian, but from what is *truly* Christian: from the Christian message itself, from a Christian faith that is not merely believed but actually lived, from *being* a Christian. But here a question arises which must form the theme of our next section.

3.

Why *Christian* Commitment?

Why be a Christian in particular? Permit me to reflect a little, and not attempt to produce a quick answer to such a great question of principle.

Recent events in Israel, India or one or other of the Islamic countries, have made many people realise afresh that, just as for a Jew or a Moslem, so for us Christians, it cannot be entirely un-important that we were born into a particular tradition of belief and community of values, and that we remain positively or negatively influenced by it, whether we like it or not. The situation is like that of the family, where, in the same way, it cannot be entirely irrelevant whether one has maintained contact or has broken it off, in anger or indifference.

Here both non-Christians and former Christians can perhaps understand the many Christians who, even though they are no less intelligent and critical, and even though they also oppose rigid Christian traditions and institutions which make it difficult to be a Christian, still do not want to give up living within the great and good Christian tradition, formed through the history of some twenty centuries. For this great and good tradition does still exist.

So, *why am I a Christian?*

○ First of all, simply because—despite all my criticisms and concerns—I can nevertheless feel fundamentally positive about a tradition that is significant for me; a tradition in which I live, side by side with so many others, past and present.

○ Because I would not dream of confusing the great Christian tradition with the present structures of the church, nor leaving a definition of true Christian values to its present administrators.

○ In brief, because—despite my violent objections to what is *called* Christian—I find in Christianity a basic orientation on the questions of the great Whence and Whither, Why and Wherefore, of humanity and the world: a basic orientation for my individual and social self. And at the same time I find in these things a spiritual home on which I do not want to turn my back, any more than I want in politics to turn my back on democracy, which in its own way has been, and is, no less misused and abused than Christianity. But admittedly, all this only hints at the decisive factor. I must make myself clearer still.

There are in fact many non-Christians or former Christians who say that they *would* believe in such a great Whence and Whither, they would believe in an Absolute or Supreme Being, a Deity, or 'God'; that atheism leaves them intellectually and emotionally unsatisfied. But they have little idea of what to do about this 'God', scarcely know what or who God is, or what he is like. In this sense, if they are not atheists they are at least agnostics.

Now this does not totally surprise me. I certainly do not want to belittle the God of the philosophers, or the God of a general religiosity, of whom agnostics generally speak. I do not want to declare this God is an idol fabricated by humanity, as some Protestant theology has done for a long time. How could I do so, when I consider Aristotle, Plato and Plotinus, Descartes, Spinoza and Leibniz, Kant and Hegel? For it is still a great thing for a human being to know something about this great Whence and Whither, Why and Wherefore, of humanity and the world; something about the great mystery of reality; and thus to have a certain basic orientation. But I would suggest that it is not very easy to live with this still-hidden mystery, with this abstract God of the philosophers; to know what or who he is, or what he is like. This God is a God without a countenance. He is 'the unknown God', the *theos agnostos* of the Acts of the Apostles, and he thus rightly remains the God of the agnostics. This at any rate is so unless, like the great philosophers of modern times (and also their atheistic opponents) we allow ourselves to be influenced by the Christian idea of God, which is present everywhere, even today.

Yet, looking more closely at that more philosophical or generally religious orientation: if we are to speak in this way of God as the great Whence, the cause of all causes, and the great Whither, the end of all ends, how am I really to know what is concealed in the cause and what awaits us at the end? Might not the end perhaps be a dark abyss, and not a place of illumination? Might not the basic support be an enticing illusion, and not a sustaining foundation? Could not the ultimate end be a definitive breakdown, and not the ultimate fulfilment? How am I to know whether the central sense of things for myself and the world will not ultimately turn out to be nonsense, the central value ultimately valueless? Such doubts are truly justified and make the consideration of a commitment to a system of essential Christian values difficult.

What and who is the God who is to provide my essential values? What is he like? In the light of the Old and New Testament I know an answer to this question. The God of the Judeo-Christian faith does not remain abstract and undetermined, like the God of the philosophers. He is concrete and determined: not hidden, but revealed in the history of the people of Israel and of Jesus Christ. And, unlike the God of the philosophers and scholars—to take up Pascal's contrast—this God of Abraham, Isaac and Jacob, the God of Jesus Christ, is not enigmatic, like the Egyptian sphinx, the strangler of passers-by. Nor is this God ambivalent, equivocal, two-faced, like the Roman God Janus, for example. Nor is he capricious, incalculable, like Tyche-Fortuna, who as the goddess of happiness and unhappiness guides the course of the world.

No, the God of the Judeo-Christian faith unambiguously proves to be a God, not *against humanity* but *for humanity*. 'Immanuel: God with us.' A God who should mean for human beings not—as is often represented by supposedly Christian teachers—fear, but security, not unhappiness but happiness, not death but life. Even in the Old Testament (despite some still mythically pagan features) not a slave-owner but a God of the exodus from Egypt, a God of liberation, of mercy, of salvation, of grace. A God beside whom there are no other gods. This one and only God is that one very last, very first reality which, together with Christians and Jews, Moslems also worship in Allah—a fact which was not unimportant for the Camp David agreement and the recent strivings for peace in the Middle East. He is the reality which Hindus also seek in Brahma and Buddhists in the Absolute Dharma (Nirvana), as do the Chinese in heaven or in the Tao. For Jews and Christians this one true God is not the unknown God. He is the good God, the God who looks on human beings with kindness, the God in whom men and women can place an absolute and unreserved trust even in doubt, suffering and sin, in all personal distress and all social affliction—the God in fact in whom we can place our faith.

This is certainly the biblical God, but the biblical God perceived in the new view of the world according to Copernicus, Galileo and Darwin. A God who, as the all-embracing and all-pervasive God of the world, is certainly not a person in the way that a human being is a person. What determines every individual human existence is not an individual person like other persons. He is not a super-ego or a Big Brother. God bursts apart the concept of person; God is more than a person.

But conversely, a God who is the foundation of the personal nature of human beings cannot himself be a-personal either. He is not sub-personal. God also bursts apart the concept of the impersonal; God is not less than a person either.

Even mathematicians and scientists had to get used to paradoxical thinking. Niels Bohr's concept of complementarity offers itself as an example here. In quantum mechanics, it depends on the question that is asked whether the answer in an experiment is expressed in terms of 'wave' or 'corpuscle'; and in the same way, in philosophical and theological discussion, it depends on the way the question is put whether, in answer to a particular question, God might be described as 'personal' or 'a-personal'. But the fact that God is fundamentally neither personal nor a-personal depends upon the incomparable nature of God. He is in fact both at the same time, and might therefore properly be called 'super-personal'.

But for our biblical faith and our Christian values today, the decisive thing is that, even though this God is 'super-personal', he is still a genuine partner who is kind and absolutely reliable, *a partner to whom we can speak*. Of course we can only talk about this God, and talk to him, in metaphors and images, in ciphers and symbols. But we can nonetheless communicate with him with human words—how else? And it is obviously on this basis that the possibility of prayer and worship depends—a possibility which, it seems to me, is enormously important, particularly for us modern human beings and our essential Christian values—which of course should not be purely intellectual. For in simple prayer and genuine worship even modern men and women can find certain values at a wholly different depth of their existence, and can truly experience where we come from, where we are, and where we are going.

Today Christians no longer have a naive belief in God, which suggests an answer to some other difficulties in the way of the Christian faith, especially scientific ones.

One difficulty is the idea of God as *the 'Creator' of heaven and earth*. Here we have to remember that the question about the final Whence of the world and human beings—the question of what there was before the Big Bang and before there was any hydrogen, the great question of why there is something instead of nothing—is a fundamentally human question. The scientist cannot supply the answer, because it lies beyond the horizon of experience. But for that very reason, he cannot sweep the question aside as irrelevant or pointless either. In trying to give an answer, it is important to remember that the creation accounts in the Bible do not intend to offer scientific information about the way the universe came into being. What they do intend to show is what we have to call a testimony of faith about the ultimate Whence of the universe, a testimony which science can neither confirm nor refute: at the beginning of the world is God. And in saying this, these biblical testimonies are stressing that God is the origin of everything and everybody; that he is not therefore in competition with any evil or demonic counter-principle; that consequently the world, as a whole and in all its individual parts—matter, the human body and sexuality included—are in principle good; indeed that human beings are the consummation of the creation process and the centre of the cosmos, and that God's creation is already a sign of his gracious commitment to the world and to men and women—which means something of decisive importance for our lives, thoughts and actions.

A second difficulty is the idea of God as *the one who 'guides' history*. How are we to understand this? If God exists, he certainly does not act in the world as someone or something that is finite and relative. He acts as the Infinite in the finite and as the Absolute in the relative. And I would add that God does not act on, or into, the world from above or outside as Unmoved Mover. As the most real and dynamic of realities he works from the inside, in the world's evolutionary process, which he makes possible, rules over and completes. He does not act on the world externally; he acts in the world itself, in and with human beings and things. Does this mean that he intervenes? The answer is that he does not intervene in the way that people have often thought. He does not merely act at a few, specially important points or crises in the affairs of the world. He is not a trouble-shooter. No, he acts as the creative and complete, fundamental sustainer and support. He therefore guides the world as the one who is both immanent in that world and superior to it, omnipresent and omnipotent, with complete respect for the natural laws at whose point of origin he himself is. He is the all-comprehending and all-pervading meaning and end of everything in the world and the whole process of world history. He 'throws dice'— but according to particular laws, as quantum mechanics and microbiology make clear. His absolute liberty does not restrict the relative liberty of human beings, but makes that liberty possible, empowering and sustaining it.

A third difficulty is the concept of God as *the 'perfecter' of the world and human beings*. One thing is clear. There is not an unequivocal scientific description or projection of the future of humanity and the universe. And I would add that none of the biblical narratives and images about the end of the world have the authority of scientific statements. We have to understand them as testimonies of faith about the Whither of the universe which, again, science can neither confirm nor refute: at the end of the world is God. Just as he is the alpha, so he is the omega. We can therefore dispense with any attempt to harmonise biblical statements and various scientific theories about the beginning and the end. The biblical testimony understands the end on an essentially different level—as the completion of God's activity in his creation. That means: what is at the world's end, as at its beginning, is not the Nothingness which explains nothing, but God. And this end must not simply be equated with a cosmic catastrophe and the sudden end of human history. What is old, transient, imperfect and evil will indeed be ended: but this end must be understood as ultimate completion and fulfilment.

The 'yes' to God is neither a cloudy emotion nor a rational proof. Human beings are faced with an alternative. They have to decide whether they are prepared to assume, in their lives and in the history of mankind and the world, that there is ultimately no basis, no support and no meaning—or that everything has after all a fundamental basis, a support and a meaning; that, to put it more concretely, there is a creator, a guide and a fulfiller. We can mistrust the basis, support and meaning of reality and say 'no' to it. Or we can trust, and say 'yes' to a God. The 'yes' to God is therefore a matter of trust—though the trust is in itself a quite reasonable trust. There is no rational proof for such an act of trust, but there are certainly many reasonable grounds. For only a trusting 'yes' to a fundamental basis, support and meaning can answer the question about the foundation, support and meaning of the world, and the ultimate meaning of our own lives. Only a trusting 'yes' can give human beings ultimate certainty, security—and in fact a genuine system of essential values. In this light, only the 'yes' is fundamentally reasonable, not the 'no', which leads to ultimate meaninglessness.

Truly we do not need—as many people fear—to

be irrational when we want to orientate ourselves in faith towards God, the Christian God. On the contrary, by believing in God the understanding really 'sees reason'! And the God of the philosophers, who appeals more to some people, is by no means abolished in the process: in the God of Jews and Christians he is what German calls, in a word with a wonderful triple sense, *aufgehboben*— he is affirmed, negated and transcended in one; affirmed, relativised and infinitely elevated. This God, I believe, is what we can call 'the more divine God'. He is the God before whom modern men and women, who have become so critical, need not renounce their reason. He is the God before whom they can again 'pray and sacrifice, fall on their knees in awe, make music and dance', to take the words with which Heidegger once formulated his hope. And so my first, fundamental answer to the question about essential Christian values is this: I know what I can rely on and will rely on, because *I believe in this living God.*

We all have a personal God: a supreme value by which we regulate everything, to which we orientate ourselves, for which if need be we sacrifice everything. And if this is not the true God, then it is some kind of idol, an old or a new one— money, career, sex or pleasure—none of them evil things in themselves, but enslaving for those for whom they become God. Orientation to the one true God, to the sole Absolute, liberates us from all these things and permits us to use them, to express ourselves as human beings with them. Orientation towards the one true God thus makes a human being truly free in this world. But in all this we are speaking very generally. We must continue our reflections and speak more precisely: where do I get my commitment to essential Christian values from?

4.

Where Do I Get My Christian Commitment from?

It is not a secret. I get it from the one whose name is so readily suppressed in Christian party programmes, and who is so readily respected merely as 'honorary chairman' without any real influence. I get these essential Christian values from Jesus of Nazareth, who is a historical figure and not a myth, and who is for that very reason the Christ who is authoritative in all things for Christians of all times. He proclaimed the one and only God, who had already spoken and been addressed in the history of the people of Israel, in the experiences of men and women; he proclaimed this God with a human face, as living and close. In his whole life and in everything he did he made this face of God shine out. When Jesus spoke of this God and acted in his name, he made clear what was vague in the Old Testament, made what seemed ambiguous there unambiguous. The one true God of Israel is now understood in a new way. We might sum it up by saying that he is understood as the Father of the Prodigal Son, indeed as the

Father of all the lost, not simply as the Father of the devout and those who were righteous from the very beginning.

This God, as Jesus proclaimed him, is not—as has often been taught to children—an all too masculine, arbitrary, legal-minded God, a kind of martinet, a God without maternal features. He is not a God created in the image of kings, tyrants and dictators. This God really is—and I beg you to take the word not in its superficial meaning, but in its deepest sense—the loving God who is my Mother too: that is, he is the God of love who for all his justice, commits himself unreservedly to all human beings, to all their needs and hopes (which is also important for questions about sexual morality). He is a God who does not always merely demand, but gives; who does not oppress, but liberates; who does not make people ill or poison their lives, but heals them. He is a God who spares those who fall—and who does not fall? A God who forgives instead of condemning, liberates instead of punishing, makes grace rule instead of law; who rejoices more over the repentance of one sinner than over ninety-nine just people. He is therefore a God who prefers the Prodigal Son to the one who stayed at home, the tax collector to the Pharisee, the Samaritan heretics to the orthodox, the prostitutes and adulterers to their self-righteous judges. As you see, this preaching of Jesus was offensive and scandalous, not only for that time in history but for today as well, particularly since it was accompanied by an equally offensive and scandalous practice: not excommunication, but communication—even communion! He sat down—he even sat down at table—with the despised and the failures, 'sinners' of every kind.

It is obvious that this God's name of Father is not merely an echo of the experience of fatherhood, masculinity, strength and power in this world. This is not a God as seen by the former theologian, and later atheist, Feuerbach: a God of the hereafter at the expense of the here and now, at the expense of human beings and their true greatness. Nor is this a God such as Karl Marx criticised: a God of the rulers, of unjust social conditions, of deformed consciousness and of false consolation. Nor is this the God rejected by Nietzsche: a God engendered by resentment, a God of pitiable weaklings. Nor is this the God rejected by Freud and a number of psychoanalysts: a tyrannical super-ego, the false image of infantile needs, a God of obsessive ritual arising from a guilt complex, a father complex or an Oedipus complex.

No, this God is a different God: a God who sets himself above the formal, logical, merciless correctness of the law and proclaims a 'better' righteousness, and may even justify a transgressor of the law; a God for whom the commandments exist for the sake of the human person, and not the human person for the sake of the commandments; a God who does not overthrow the existing legal order and the whole social system, but who tempers it for humanity's sake; and a God who consequently wants to have the barriers of categorisation between good people and bad, friends and foes, neighbours and strangers, workers and unemployed, removed. How?—by humility, self-denial, love, forgiveness without end, service regardless of reward, sacrifice without compensation. In this way God puts himself on the side of the disadvantaged, the underprivileged, the oppressed, the weak, the poor and the sick, and even—unlike the self-righteous—on the side of the irreligious, the immoral and the godless. God is kind, wonderfully kind, to human beings.

It was for this God and his wonderful kindness that Jesus pleaded. For him he spoke, fought, suffered and was executed. And at this point, of course, the question always arises: did it not all end with his death? The cautious answer can at first be one that even the non-Christian can accept. It is a fact of world history that Jesus' death was not the end of everything but only the beginning: that his first community, in a truly reckless fashion, proclaimed him—the heretical teacher, false prophet, seducer of the people, blasphemer, allegedly condemned by God—to be God's Messiah, the Christ, Lord, Son of man, Son of God. And why? According to the New Testament sources, they were convinced—and only this conviction explains the emergence of Christianity at all—that Jesus had died, not into nothingness, but into God. That means that Jesus is living: living through, with and in God. What for? For us: as hope, as obligation, for our essential values.

Ever since then both Christians and non-Christians have been faced with a clear alternative in the direction they lead their lives.

There is the possibility that we die into nothingness. I would not deny my respect for anyone who adopts this position. This is a view which sometimes demands heroism, and can certainly not be refuted. Of course no one has proved it positively either. There has never yet been anyone who could prove that we die into nothingness, that all our living, labouring, loving and suffering ends in nothingness and was ultimately for nothing. And to me this possibility does not seem reasonable; under no circumstances does it seem reasonable.

This is the other possibility: that we die into an absolute reality which we call God, because we still have no better name for it. This alternative too cannot be proved; nor of course can it be refuted. Here every human being is faced with a decision that no one can take away. We have no rational proof for eternal life. But—as I have already said—we do have reasonable grounds. We can commit ourselves to this in enlightened, reasonable trust. Truly, not to console ourselves with the promise of a hereafter, but to set ourselves all the more decisively in the here and now, in this life, in this present-day society. And that we do not die into nothingness but into God seems to me more reasonable; it seems more reasonable under any circumstances. Think: if God really exists and if he really is God, he cannot be merely the God of the beginning, but must also be the God of the end. Then he is our Finisher as well as our Creator. And it is he alone, the Creator and Preserver of the cosmos and of human beings, who can be expected to have one more word to say, even in dying and at death, beyond the frontiers of all that has hitherto been experienced: to have the last word, just as he had the first. If I seriously believe in an eternal, living God, I believe also in God's eternal life, in my own eternal life. So if I begin my profession of faith with belief in 'God the almighty, the creator' I may very well finish it with belief in 'life everlasting'.

A firm faith of this kind changes even this present life completely. It enables us to live quite differently, with more meaning, more responsibility, with greater involvement. In fact it enables us to live in accordance with the standard of this Christ. With his proclamation, the way he lived, and his fate, He became the standard for those who believe in him: the standard for their relations with their fellow human beings, with society, and above all with God. To put it briefly, for believers the true man Jesus of Nazareth has therefore always been the real and clear revelation of the one God: his Messiah, his Christ, his image and his son.

But it is in this very way that he is a truly human being, *the* true human being. Through his proclamation, his behaviour, his whole destiny, he provided *a model of being human* which, if we commit ourselves trustingly to it, enables us again and again to discover and to realise the meaning of our own being human, of our freedom, of our life: in our own existence and in living with our fellow human beings. Confirmed by God in the resurrection, he thus represents for us the enduring, reliable, ultimate standard of what being human means. What has surely become plain in recent theological disputes is that Christology, or a theory about Christ, may be important, particularly for theologians and bishops, but faith in Christ and discipleship are the essentials. *Being* a Christian is the important thing. And it is he who makes that possible for me—he, the Christ of God, who is identical with the historical human being, Jesus of Nazareth.

So that is how I would answer the question 'where do I get my Christian commitment from?'. I know what I can rely on, what I can hold on to, *because I believe in this Christ Jesus*. But in saying this I am also faced with the question which must not be passed over under any circumstances: 'what does all this mean in practice?'.

5.

What Does Christian Commitment Mean in Practice?

Here I can give no more than indications of the general direction we should take. Let me say at the very beginning that it would be presumptuous in this brief reflection to suggest an approach to every important and topical problem—not least because for different people different problems are important and topical. What I am concerned about here is fundamental Christian thinking and awareness: a commitment to the essential Christian values. Of course these must exert their influence on all the practical questions of the individual and society. Being a Christian must profoundly influence a person's approach, for example, to the problems of war and peace, violence and non-violence, the struggle for power, the pressure towards more and more consumption; it must make itself felt in education; it must show itself in service for others. But here I shall confine myself to the general principles of Christian practice. Of course one important point must be made. What I indicate or hint at here is not just what is often reproachfully called 'pure theory'; it is the theory behind a practice which is actually lived out day by day by an untold number of people in our churches—or perhaps one should say that an untold number of people try to live in this way, as best they can. And because of this, I believe our churches remain fundamentally Christian, in spite of all the merely nominal Christianity there is within them.

Marx is master and teacher for Marxists, and Freud for Freudians. Jesus of Nazareth is certainly also master and teacher for the life of Christians. But he is also essentially more than that. As the one who was killed and raised to life, he is for believers the living authoritative embodiment of his cause. In all that he is, in all that he said, did and suffered, he personifies the cause of God and the cause of humanity. And so he calls us to discipleship. For some this is too lofty a word, and in its challenge almost alarming. But do not let us misunderstand what discipleship means. Certainly the living Christ does not call merely for adoration without practical commitment, nor simply for us to say 'Lord, Lord' or 'Son of God, Son of God'. But neither does he call us to literal imitation. It would be presumptuous to want to imitate him. No, he calls for personal discipleship, not in imitation but in correlation, in *correspondence*. That means that I commit myself to him and pursue my own way in accordance with his direction—for each of us has his or her own path to follow. It is not that we must. We are not compelled. Making his way our own was understood from the very beginning as a very great opportunity, not a 'must' but a 'may', not a law to be obeyed slavishly but an unexpected chance and a true gift; that is—and this word too has often been misunderstood—a genuine grace on which we are *permitted* to rely. A grace that presupposes no more than this one thing: that I grasp it confidently and try to adapt my life to it.

All Christian churches ought to know this: *it is this Jesus Christ himself*, who personifies his cause, who is the specifically Christian, the decisively Christian fact, and not some 'Christian' or Western idea in the abstract, some kind of ethical postulate, a devout turn of mind, an abstract principle or an ecclesiastical or theological system. He himself, this specific Jesus as the living Christ, is for believers in all situations the ultimate authority on whom we may rely.

This basic model of essential values in individual and social life does not of course aim merely at providing internal, spiritual and mental comfort. It involves a conversion of the heart: a new attitude which can change the world! It makes actually possible what so many are calling for today, with the prevailing lack of direction, lack of norms, lack of meaning; with the prevailing drug addiction, criminality and violence. It makes actually possible what is so important for both the religion *and* politics of Christians, for their social and economic policies, for their educational and development policies. If I can set it out: this Jesus Christ and his Spirit, who is *the energy and power of God himself*, makes actually possible

○ new awareness: He makes possible a standpoint beside which many others can be judged. He requires a new, more humane attitude to life, and a new life-style itself. As individuals and together, we may and can live differently, more authentically, more humanely, when we have this Christ Jesus before us as a specific example for our fundamental relationships with others, society, the world of God. This new attitude gives us identity and integrity in our individual lives, and a confident independence and motivation to act in today's society.

○ new motivations: From his 'theory' and 'practice' we can deduce new motives for individual and social action. In his light, it is possible to answer those questions with which we started out and which are so difficult to answer purely rationally: why we should not act in one particular way but in another, why we should not be wicked and inhumane but should be humane and good, why we should not hate but love, why we should not promote violence and war but should affirm non-violence and promote peace. In the light of

Jesus Christ it is possible to answer even the question which Freud, with all his brilliant insight, could not answer: why we should still be honest, considerate and kind whenever possible, even if this is to our disadvantage and we are made to suffer through the carelessness and brutality of others.

○ new attitudes: In his Spirit we can develop and maintain new, reliable insights and attitudes. We can find in him help—not only occasionally but dependably—to form new attitudes with all the required subtleties, which are capable of guiding individual and social behaviour successfully: attitudes of unpretentious commitment to our fellow human beings, identification with the underprivileged and opposition to unjust institutions; attitudes of gratitude, freedom, magnanimity, unselfishness and joy, as well as consideration, pardon and service; attitudes which prove themselves in difficult situations, in preparedness for sacrifice, in the fullness of self-giving and in renunciation—sometimes even when not absolutely necessary in dedication to a greater cause.

○ new action: By his Spirit we are enabled to act on a larger or smaller scale, not only in general programmes for social change, but also in detailed, practical ways for the benefit of individuals and society.

○ new aims: Through his Spirit there comes what
    so many people miss today—the meaning and
    ultimate purpose of our life and our history in
    that last and first reality which is the
    consummation of humanity through God's
    kingdom. It is precisely this meaning and this
    purpose that permit us to live our present,
    earthly lives differently: and that means life not
    only as a history of successes, but also as a
    history of suffering, for the individual and for
    humanity as a whole.

   This last point needs to be expressed more
exactly. Non-Christians often describe themselves
as humanists, but we Christians too are no less
humanists. The crucial test of both non-Christian
humanism and Christian humanism lies in their
capacity to deal with the negative aspect of reality.
While it is easy enough to say that we approve of
everything that is human, humane, true, good and
beautiful, what if we continually come up against
the inhuman, inhumane, untrue, bad and ugly, in
our individual lives and in society, and if we cannot
simply talk these negative things out of existence?
How then is the negative side to be dealt with?
   It is only now, and with the utmost caution, that
I introduce the idea that has been misused by so
many in order to enslave humanity and to deceive
with false consolation: *the cross*, or, rather, *the One*

crucified, enables us to cope even with the negative element. Who can deny that human existence—under whatever social and economic system, and even after all reforms and revolutions—is and remains an existence shot through with pain, anxiety, guilt, suffering, sickness and death and is in this sense a thwarted and unsatisfactory thing? But this frustrated existence of ours acquires an indisputable meaning in the light of the resurrection of Jesus. For no suffering in the world can dismiss the offer of meaning—it is no more than an offer—presented in the suffering and death of the One who was raised to life. For the person who trusts in God, even the negative, even the greatest danger, the utmost loneliness, futility, nullity, guilt and emptiness are encompassed by a God who identifies himself with humanity, even if we do not perceive this at the time. We are not under any illusions here: there is no way of ignoring the negative things. What we are given is the ability to endure without self-pity, a way through, a future to which our own life and suffering leads. This does not mean seeking out the negative, but enduring it; not merely enduring it, but fighting against it.

In the Spirit of the One crucified, a struggle against all the negative aspects of the condition of human life and their causes is possible at a very much deeper level by both individuals and society.

That is

○ a struggle to ensure respect for human dignity against all animosity towards humanity—and even to the point of love for one's enemies;

○ a struggle for freedom against all oppression—and even to the point of selfless service;

○ a struggle for justice against all injustice—and even to the point of voluntarily surrendering one's rights;

○ a struggle against all selfishness—and even to the point of giving up things we own;

○ a struggle for peace against all strife—and even to the point of infinite reconciliation.

Why then am I committed to the essential Christian values? Here is a third answer, which gives a last clarification: I know what I can rely on, what I can hold on to, because I believe in *the Spirit of Jesus Christ, who is alive today, who is the Spirit of God himself, who is the Holy Spirit*. This living Spirit enables me and countless others to be truly human: not only to act in a truly human way, but also to suffer; not only to live, but also to die—because in everything, both positive and negative, in all happiness and unhappiness, we are sustained by God and can sense our fellow human beings. And in this sense we as Christians represent not just any kind of humanism but a truly *radical* humanism: a humanism that goes to the roots, since it is able to embody, not merely the true, the good and the beautiful, whatever is human and humane, but also the untrue, the bad and the ugly, whatever is all-too-human and even inhuman. These things too it is able, suffering and struggling, to embrace positively.

6.

Opportunities for Christians

There are opportunities that spring from being a Christian. Whether believer or unbeliever, Christian or non-Christian, no one will deny that such a commitment to the essential values provides an answer to the 'crisis' of values with which we began: a commitment to essential values which—taking their definition from the biblical 'trinitarian' language about the Father, the Son and the Spirit—is able to give to our individual and social life a new direction, a new dimension, a new support, a new meaning; a way between revolution and servility, between hypercritical radicalism and complacent conformity—a way for the younger generation especially. What each individual actually does with this sort of answer depends of course on his own personal decision. There can be no pressure or compulsion here. But this much is certain:

○ The more human beings—man or woman, workers, clerks or university graduates—accept these essential values, so much freer, so much more open, human, philanthropic do they become.

○ The more older people hold on to these values, the more sympathetically will they also approach the younger generation, with the utmost degree of understanding and yet with firmness, having to make no false concessions.

○ The more younger people engage with this alternative, with a Christian way of life and a Christian life-style, the more will they overcome the unfruitful, sullen frustration, discontent and animosity that is so widespread today; and the more will they discover a genuine autonomy and scope for freedom, so that with a new sense of reality they can do their utmost for their fellow human beings.

○ The more a political party (whether it calls itself a 'Christian' party or not) allows itself, tacitly or openly, to be animated by such a Spirit towards basic rights, attitudes and norms, the more will it achieve its aim of being in close contact with the needs of the people, as citizens and as human beings. It will not only be in power, or striving for power; it will be truly at the service of men and women.

○ The more a church—whether Catholic, Protestant or Orthodox—is not only called Christian but behaves in a Christian way, the more will it become open, welcoming, hospitable, truly credible; the more easily will it be able to solve the internal church problems to which I referred so critically at the beginning; and the more will it truly give hope to men and women.

○ The more a society—whether it is formally Christian, or pluralistic in the modern way—is sustained by people, institutions and churches, for whom Christianity has again come to mean something, the more will it become a society not only orientated towards happiness but, more solidly, towards truth.

HOW DO WE PERSEVERE?

'Will any one of you, who has a servant ploughing
or keeping sheep, say to him when he has come in
from the field, "Come at once and sit down at
table"? Will he not rather say to him, "Prepare
supper for me and gird yourself and serve me, till I
eat and drink, and afterwards you shall eat and
drink"? Does he thank the servant because he did
what was commanded? So you also, when you
have done all that is commanded you, say, "We
are unworthy servants. We have only done what
was our duty".' (Lk 17:7–10).

1963—the Year of Visions

It is already more than twenty years since I went to
the United States for the first time—in 1963. It was
a year of hope for America, and not only for her
churches but also for churches throughout the
world. It was a year of hope for everyone.

For everybody who followed the events closely,
1963 was a year of great visions. There was an

American Preisdent, John F. Kennedy, who had visions of 'new frontiers'—new and bold frontiers of progress, social justice and peace for America and the world. And there was at that time no anti-Americanism in Europe, but a great deal of co-operation and even enthusiasm.

There was also a pope, John XXIII, who had opened the Second Vatican Council in the previous year and had shaken his Church awake with the religious vision of an *aggiornamento*. The Catholic Church was to be renewed in accordance with the Gospel. Christians and Jews were to discover a new relationship with each other and Christianity, and the world religions were to enter into a positive dialogue. He was the first Pope who had ever spoken in encyclicals about human rights and world peace.

We Catholic theologians went to work at that time with great passion. We had been appointed by Pope John XXIII as advisers to the council—I was at that time the youngest of them—and we wanted to help to give a concrete theological foundation to the vision and see it through. We were invited to travel and get to know the world Church. I was thirty-five years old when I went to America for the first time. I gave many lectures, mainly on the theme of 'the Church and freedom', from the East to the West coast. It was a theme that seemed to interest and excite my listeners because it was unprecendented in Catholic circles.

1963 was certainly a year of visions, but perhaps it was also a year of illusions? No, it was not. An enormous amount had been accomplished and neither the Catholic Church nor the other churches have been the same since—neither in their worship, nor in their theology, nor in their church order. For the Catholic Church, the Middle Ages and the anti-Protestant Counter-Reformation had finally come to an end. New things had been achieved, but there have also been disappointments.

The Disappointments

Six months later, at Whitsun 1963, John XXIII died; and in November 1963 President Kennedy was murdered. The men in whom we had placed our hope were dead.

But we remained with our visions in our minds and our hope in our hearts. And since that time we have never been free of the conviction

○ that it is possible for a new society to exist—a more peaceful, a more just and a more human society;

○ that it is possible for a renewed Church and a renewed theology to exist—a Church and a theology which are more in accordance with the hopes and needs of people today and with the Gospel of Jesus Christ.

Far too much has happened in the meantime—enough to burst these dreams like soap bubbles:

○ in politics: Vietnam, Watergate, the oil crisis, the economic recession, worldwide unemployment and rearmament by the world powers;
○ in the Church: fear of the spirit of the Council on the part of the popes and the Curia, who began putting on the brake and eventually stopped all further progress.

Paul VI became more and more sombre and ceased to radiate the hope that had illuminated his predecessor. The world breathed again when a pope laughed again. But John Paul I, 'the laughing pope' died after only thirty days in office, torn between the old tendency and the new. All the more hope was therefore placed in John Paul II, the first non-Italian to sit on the throne of Peter for hundreds of years. But Rome only showed herself to be open to the outside world in the social questions that did not directly concern the Church itself, and closed up on all questions of Church renewal, Christian freedom and spiritual creativity.

Many people, both in the Catholic Church and outside it, cannot resolve the contradictions in the policy of the Roman hierarchy

○ that poverty in the world is, on the one hand, firmly opposed, but that, on the other, the contraceptive pill is forbidden as immoral;

○ that human rights are proclaimed, but that the Church's own theologians are intimidated, disciplined or even dismissed, and the clergy forbidden to marry;

○ that there is openness to the world, but that women are discriminated against in the Church and are not even tolerated as lowly servers at the altar, let alone permitted to be ordained;

○ that ecumenical visits are made to Germany, Switzerland, Canterbury and Constantinople, but that Catholic Marianism is cultivated again in an extreme form, and Catholic infallibility cannot be questioned.

So there have been twenty years of hopes and disappointments, successes and setbacks.

○ Many committed men and women have left the Church, disappointed, resigned and even despairing;

○ tens of thousands of priests have had to give up their office because they wanted to marry;

○ tens of thousands of nuns have left because they have not been permitted to have a new creative Christian life-style;

○ in many churches throughout the world there has been a frightening decline not only in attendance at public worship, but also in the number of baptisms and church marriages;

O many parishes no longer have a parish priest because of the lack of candidates for the priesthood;

O many of my own friends have also left and have called on me and others to come with them: 'Leave the Church to its own devices. You can do other things outside the Church. People like you do not fit into such a Church'.

Yes, you can be confronted with this fundamental question if you live and work in this Church. I was confronted with it in a very dramatic form some years ago and many of us have been confronted with it in more or less dramatic forms. What is it that keeps a person in this Church? Why should we persevere at all?

Why We Persevere

Why do we persevere in a Church, in a society, wherever we happen to be

O if we see how little the Church and society are really renewed because of it;

O if the wind has changed directions and is now blowing in our faces;

O if we are no longer swimming with the current, but against it, and our strength is declining;

○ if our ideas are ignored, or are rejected and even
  encounter hostility and hatred;
○ if our Christianity and Church membership are
  denied by others, and any form of defamation is
  regarded as satisfactory argument?

I admit that not everyone is placed in the same
position of dramatic conflict and not everyone is
obliged to say yes or no within a few days.

But is there anyone who has not experienced
fundamental disappointments and defeats?
Disappointments and defeats that have made
them ask, in the circle in which they live, at their
place of work, in their Church, in politics, in state
affairs, this radical question: why do we persevere?
Why do we continue as we began? Why do we
cling to the vision that we had when we were
young and idealistic, instead of accepting the
'realism' and 'cynicism' of advancing years?

There are general reasons why we should
persevere. These are reasons to which even all non-
Christians would assent. They are, however we
may justify them, maxims. We persevere

○ because we ought not to betray the dreams of
  our youth;
○ because our vision is not made wrong merely
  because by chance there is a change of
  government and we suddenly find ourselves in
  the opposition;

○ because we cannot change a fundamental attitude in life as we might change a coat;
○ because firmness of character, holding on to convictions and upright behaviour, are not to be regarded as fashionable attitudes, or snobbish, or vulgar, or cosmetic luxuries, but as fundamental moral obligations.

These are, I admit, good reasons, but yet none of them in my opinion goes quite to the root of the question. As a Christian who tries to follow Christ seriously, perhaps I can add something more personal:

I persevere

○ because we can still enjoy successes, even if they are difficult to measure quantitatively;
○ because, in the light of Jesus' message, the small size of a group, the limited means, the seeming ineffectiveness of the activity and the setbacks encountered in the work should not be seen as signs of failure;
○ because again and again I am given everything that I need to hold out and am therefore not tried beyond my strength;
○ because, seen in the light of the suffering and crucified Jesus, it is precisely in impotence that power, in weakness that strength, in smallness that greatness, and in humility that self-consciousness can be manifested;

○ because we can therefore hope against hope, even in the Church.

Many people ask: 'even in the Church?'

Is There Reason for Hope even in the Church?

Despite all the reaction and restoration on the part of Rome, we can, I believe, be sure

○ that the future of the Church has already begun;
○ that the will to renew is not limited only to certain small groups;
○ that the recent unnecessary polarisations of opinion within the Church can be overcome;
○ that the best priests, members of religious communities and bishops give their consent now, as they have done in the past, to a radical renewal, and are promoting it;
○ that we men and women in the Catholic Church are supported by many creative forces in the other churches.

But for me what is even more important is that we can hope

○ because the Church cannot put back all the clocks in the world; cannot hold up the world's development and return to the Middle Ages or the Counter-Reformation;

○ because the power of the Gospel of Jesus Christ will prove in the long run to be stronger than all human incompetence, fear and insincerity and more forceful than all our foolishness, weakness and cynicism.

That is why, in my opinion, we can persevere, whatever place we occupy in the Church. But perhaps we would also like to know not only why we *ought* to persevere, but also *how* we are to persevere?

How Do We Persevere?

I have been asked so many times: 'How do you persevere?' It certainly requires all one's resources. I would condemn no one for not persevering. You need good health, both physically and psychologically, and a sense of humour. You need to be fairly easy-going. Above all, you need people who will not leave you alone in your hour of need, but will bear everything with you, even in ordinary everyday life. It is hardly possible to persevere on one's own.

But what if one could not preserve one's physical and psychological health, humour and trustworthy friends? A great deal could be said about this, but I will simply mention what seems to me to be most important, what would be able to sustain me and what would be for me the ultimate support, even if everything else broke down: if for one reason or another I lost my sense of humour; if I became entangled in feelings of deepest guilt; if I lost all hope of success; if I lost my health; if I lost my friends, and even my trust in other people.

What, then, for me really counts in the life of a Christian? That is the important question: what is really decisive? Success? Achievements?

Success Does not Matter!

No, even if success counts for most in our society, and everyone loves success, and nothing succeeds like success: success does not matter ultimately for the Christian! Christians are not dependent on making progress, winning, or on always being right.

This certainly does not mean that Christians are exempted from fighting for their convictions wherever they find themselves, or from persuading others. But, however important achievements may be in everyday life, in professional life and even in the Church, demonstrable achievements do not ultimately matter. Am I not capable of achieving 'wrong' of a very serious kind? Who would deny that I am? But equally, achievements of wrong do not ultimately matter to the Christian. And just as achievements do not ultimately matter, so too failure and defeat do not occupy a predominant status in my life.

63

There is something else of decisive importance. It is this: in difficult situations and even in the deepest distress and greatest guilt, I should not despair. No, I should never despair! To express this in a more positive way, I would always preserve unshakable trust: an unshakable and unconditional *faithful trust*; an unshakable and unconditional *trusting faith*. That is what was decisive for Abraham and the patriarchs of Israel: 'Abraham believed and it was reckoned to him as righteousness' (Rom 4:3); what was decisive for Mary and the first disciples: 'Blessed are you ... who believed' (Lk 1:42, 45); what was decisive for Peter, who was so humanly likeable in his pusillanimity, which enabled him to learn from Jesus: to walk on the water, without heeding the waves, with his eyes on him; what was decisive for the Apostle Paul: who impressed on his believers with an appeal to his Christ that we are justified not by our achievements, but by our faith, by our unconditional trust. And in this Paul showed the deepest understanding of Jesus, of what mattered to Jesus and of his message in the parables of the prodigal son, the pharisee and the publican, and the labourers in the vineyard. Here Paul understood what really mattered *in the case of Jesus*, in his teaching, working, struggling, suffering and finally in his death. What Paul places before himself and before us is the crucified Christ, for whom, hanging on the cross, achievements and successes no longer existed; the Christ who was justified by God alone, his Father and our Father. What the crucified Christ had revealed to him was that we are justified by faith alone.

Unworthy Servants

As a theologian and a Christian, I am firmly on the side of Karl Barth, the great Protestant theologian, who once told me that he would not point at the end to his collected theological writings for justification, or even mention his 'good intentions'. in his view, the only suitable words that he could say in the presence of his judge were: 'God, have mercy on me, a sinner'.

At the beginning and at the end we place our trust in God's grace. But is that not typically Protestant? I think it is typically *evangelical*, and I have basically only drawn upon the scriptural text 'So you also, when you have done all that is commanded you, say, "We are *unworthy servants. We have only done what was our duty*" '.

That is surely typically evangelical and, because it is typically evangelical, it is also typically catholic, as we confess in the great catholic song of praise, the *Te Deum*: '*In te, domine, speravi, non confundar in aeternum*! In you, Lord, I have placed my trust and I will not be put to shame in eternity!'.

Trusting in faith and hope like this does not

make us passive and inactive. On the contrary, it makes us more active, more responsible and more committed in the Church and in society.

Those who are critical of Christianity say: God limits people's freedom. The very opposite is true. Only by committing oneself to an infinite freedom can a person be free in a world that in all things seems only finite. Those who criticise Christianity say: God enslaves people. The very opposite is true. Only by committing oneself to God and his will can a person be set free from slavery to the powers and possessions of this world, of society and of history.

Those who are critical of Christianity say: God lets people say 'yes' and 'amen' to everything. The very opposite is true. Only his or her relationship with God enables a person to say 'no'.

Faith, then, gives us strength to act, to be free, to be decisive and to persevere. Even very small, weak faith is sufficient. Immediately before the words 'We are unworthy servants', there is a passage about the power of faith: 'The apostles said to the Lord, "Increase our faith!". And the Lord said, "If you had faith as a grain of mustard seed, you could say to this sycamine tree, 'Be rooted up and be planted in the sea' and it would obey you".' (Lk 17:5f.).

IS CHRIST DIVIDED?

'God is faithful, by whom you were called into the fellowship of the Son, Jesus Christ our Lord. I appeal to you, brethren, by the name of our Lord Jesus Christ, that all of you agree that there be no dissensions among you, but that you be united in the same mind and the same judgment. For it has been reported to me by Chloe's people that there is quarrelling among you, my brethren. What I mean is that each one of you says: "I belong to Paul" or "I belong to Apollos" or "I belong to Cephas" or "I belong to Christ".

'*Is Christ divided?* Was Paul crucified for you? Or were you baptised in the name of Paul? I thank God that I baptised none of you except Crispus and Gaius, lest anyone should say that you were baptised in my name. (I did baptise also the household of Stephanas. Beyond that, I do not know whether I baptised anyone else.) For Christ did not send me to baptise, but to preach the gospel and not with eloquent wisdom, lest the cross of Christ be emptied of its power. For the word of the cross is folly to those who are perishing, but to us who are being saved it is the power of God.' (1 Cor 1:9–18).

Church-dividing Denominations

Paul's letter is the first major document of the New Testament, written in Ephesus some twenty years after the death of Jesus to the Christian community in the great city of Corinth. Already, even then, there is talk of tensions, divisions, schisms and different denominations—in the name of Peter, Paul, Apollos and even Christ. And although we have to accept a certain anachronism, are there not parallels between this and our situation today?

First there are the Catholics, the denomination of Peter, who seems, because of his primacy, his power of the keys and his pastoral authority, to put them in the right as opposed to all other Christians.

Then there are the Orthodox, the denomination of Apollos, who has the great tradition of Greek thought on his side and has provided a more brilliant, clear and 'correct' or 'orthodox' explanation of revelation than all the others.

Then the Protestants, the denomination of Paul, who is the father of their community, the Apostle pure and simple, the unique proclaimer of the cross of Christ who has worked harder than all the others.

Finally, we should not forget the Free Churches, the denomination of Christ himself, who aim to free themselves from the oppression of the great churches with their authorities and professions of faith, to rely only on Christ as their Lord and master and to let the life of their communities be fashioned only on that basis.

And for which denomination does Paul opt? There is no doubt that Catholics would expect an allusion to Peter, who is, according to Matthew, the 'rock' on which the Church is built. But Paul passes over the name of Peter in silence, as he also tactfully passes over the name of Apollos.

What is quite astonishing, however, is that Paul also disavows his own supporters. Why? Because he does not want groups to gather around a man and make into an ideal a man who was *not* crucified for them and in whose name they were *not* baptised. They were, after all, not baptised in his name, but in the name of Christ, the one who was crucified. So even the name of Paul, who founded the community, is not permitted to be used in a denomination.

If this text contains something quintessential for ecumenical thought today, it is this: No name, no office, no authority and no speciality of any one Church should be permitted to divide the Church. What does this mean in practice?

It means that, understood in the New Testament sense, a Petrine ministry may well be a 'rock' for the Church, its unity and its cohesion, but it cannot be allowed to become simply the criterion for where the Church of Christ is.

Tradition, as understood by the Greek Orthodox, may be a very good guideline for the Church, its continuity and its permanence, but it must not become a dividing line, beyond which only heterodoxy can exist instead of orthodoxy.

Even the Bible of the Protestants who are disposed towards Paulinism may be fundamental for the Church, its faith and its profession of faith, but it should not become a quarry for stones that are used, not to build, but to throw at offenders.

Finally, even Christ the Lord, to whom a direct appeal is made in the Free Church tradition, cannot serve as a shield for those denominations who want to go into battle against other members of the one Church.

Paul confronts each one of these different denominations with its own special form, tradition and doctrine—however justified these may be in themselves—with the question that makes all special denominations seem relative: '*Is Christ divided?*'.

But what would Paul say, if he could see the way in which we Christians, all of whom are baptised in the name of the one Christ Jesus, celebrate the meal in memory of that same Jesus Christ today? If he could see how we now celebrate the *memoria Domini*, the Eucharist or celebration of thanksgiving, the *koinonia*, the communion with Christ and with each other, in a word, the *meal of unity*?

'Is Christ divided?' is, I think, what he would say to us, our denominational churches and their church leaders, who have preserved this state of separation now for as long as five hundred years in one case and nine hundred in another.

And he would add surely: 'It is precisely in this community of the meal that race, education and sex should be subsumed in Christ. For in him 'there is neither Jew nor Greek, there is neither slave nor free, there is neither male nor female' (Gal 3:28).

If, then, political and social, cultural and even sexual tensions and contradictions are quite consciously to be overcome in the celebration of the eucharistic meal, why not denominational tensions and divisions as well?

Overcoming Differences

But, from the official churches, what we hear is: 'We do not have the same understanding of the Lord's Supper or the same understanding in faith'. Certainly we do not all have the same theology, but may we not perhaps have the same faith? A great number of official documents on the increasing consensus between the confessions have been published by various churches. The joint publication that appeared in 1983, the *Dokumente wachsender Übereinstimmung*, has seven hundred pages!

Why, then, has what is contained in these documents not been put into practice? What emerges with great clarity from them is that there must be an end to all divisions in faith over our understanding of the Eucharist or the Lord's Supper. And this has, of course, been the conviction of many Christians for a very long time.

It is central to the Declaration on Convergence that was worked out over a period of twenty years by the Commission for Faith and Order of the World Council of Churches together with official representatives of the Catholic Church and officially published in Lima in 1982 under the title 'Baptism, Eucharist and Office'.

The Lima Liturgy, which was worked out by the same ecumenical Commission and celebrated there for the first time has, in the meantime, been tried out not only at the most recent Plenary Assembly of the World Council of Churches in Vancouver in collaboration with the German Catholic bishop responsible for ecumenism and many Catholic theologians, but also in many Protestant and Catholic communities in the Federal Republic of Germany.

We use this Liturgy in ecumenical celebrations especially for the eucharistic prayer, in order to make it possible for Christians of all denominations to pray, praise God, make petitions and give thanks in common. This communal 'thanksgiving' is, of course, a communal Eucharistia.

What emerges clearly from the Lima Declaration and the Lima Liturgy is that the differences that led in the sixteenth century to a division in the Church have been overcome! And what is particularly striking here is that the document has nothing at all to say about the two principal points of controversy: the use of the vernacular in the liturgy and the giving of the chalice to the laity during the eucharistic meal.

(It is worth reflecting just how many wars of religion would have been spared if Rome had only been more open four hundred and fifty years ago in those two questions; and in the question of married clergy.)

Even the dogmatic differences can be regarded as fundamentally surmountable. I would like to mention briefly only the four main points of controversy here (the 'commentaries' on these can be read in the Lima document):

○ The first controversial point is whether the Eucharist is an expiatory sacrifice or not. No informed Catholic would ever say today that the celebration of the Eucharist is a 'repetition' by the priest of the sacrifice of the cross. On the other hand, Protestants are also able to understand that it does not contradict the unique and unrepeatable character of the sacrifice of the cross when Catholics say that Jesus' unique giving of himself and expiation is 'made present' in the Eucharist.

All Christians can therefore give their consent to what is said in the Lima Declaration: 'The Eucharist is the sacrament of the unique sacrifice of Christ, who lives eternally, done in order to make intercession for us. It is the commemoration of all that God has done for the salvation of the world.'

○ The second controversial point is whether Jesus Christ is really present in the forms of bread and wine. No informed Protestant would ever be of the opinion today that Jesus' becoming present in the eucharistic meal depends simply on our faith. Nor would any informed Catholic be of the opinion that Man's faith plays no part at all in the matter of Jesus' presence in the celebration of the Eucharist.

All Christians can therefore give their consent to the Lima document when it declares that the eucharistic meal is 'the sacrament of the Body and Blood of Christ, the sacrament of his real presence … The Church confesses Christ's real, living and active presence in the Eucharist … Although Christ's real presence in the Eucharist does not depend on the faith of the individual, everyone nonetheless agrees that faith is necessary, in order to be able to distinguish Christ's Body and Blood.'

○ The third point of controversy is whether the eucharistic gifts are transformed, whether there is 'transubstantiation'. No informed Catholic would ever hold the view today that Jesus Christ's presence in the Eucharist can only be explained in one way, that is with the help of the theory of transubstantiation that was developed in the Middle Ages and the Counter-Reformation. At the same time, no informed Protestant would simply dismiss the doctrine of transubstantiation with incredulity.

All Christians, then, can give their consent to these words in the Lima document: 'In the history of the Church, various attempts have been made to understand the mystery of the real and unique presence of Christ in the Eucharist. Some have been satisfied simply to give consent to that presence, without trying to understand it. Others regard it as necessary to insist on a change brought about by the Holy Spirit and Christ's words which has the result that they are no longer ordinary bread and ordinary wine, but the Body and Blood of Christ.'

○ The fourth controversial point is who is able to 'celebrate' the Eucharist? No informed Catholic would claim today that the Eucharist is celebrated by the priest alone on behalf of the people. Similarly, no Protestant would claim that simply any Christian could celebrate the

Eucharist whenever and in whatever way he wanted to.

All Christians, however, are able to give their consent to the Lima document's declaration: 'It is Christ who invites us to the meal and presides at it ... In most churches, this presiding function is performed by an ordained office-bearer ... The minister of the Eucharist is the messenger who represents the divine initiative and who expresses the link between the local community and the other local communities in the universal Church.'

After the appearance of so many documents aiming at unification it is certainly high time that the Catholic Church should recognise Protestant office-bearers and Protestant celebrations of the Lord's Supper as valid. As long ago as at the Ecumenical Meeting in Augsburg at Whitsun 1971 at which thousands of people spontaneously practised intercommunion, the great majority of those present made their wish known to all church leaders. This was that communal celebrations of the Eucharist should be permitted for ecumenical groups and married couples belonging to different denominations, and that it should be possible for any Christian who wanted to receive communion to do so in any Christian church. Any prohibitions contrary to this should be withdrawn by the churches.

Why, then, have we still made no official

progress in this direction? Why are we still reacting—often on both sides—with narrow-mindedness, anxiety for orthodoxy, distrust and fear? Why have the Würzburg Synod and the papal visit borne no practical ecumenical results?

Go Out, You Unholy Spirit!

Anyone who has ever been engaged in ecumenical work will have experienced what I am about to describe: an ecumenical commission may consist of members of internationally recognised high calibre; they may be acknowledged experts in exegesis, history and systematic theology; and they may produce a document on unification that is theologically and linguistically almost perfect. But no practical ecumenical progress at all will be made if the true spirit is absent. And by this, I do not mean simply the spirit of friendship and collegiality, nor the 'spirit of the age', nor simply the human spirit.

No, I mean the true spirit that can counter the cast of mind that, even nine hundred years after the schism between the Western and the Eastern churches and five hundred years after the division between the Catholic and the Protestant churches in the West, maintains that

○ the time is not yet ripe for agreement, for doing away with excommunication, for restoring communion and for a communal celebration of the Eucharist and the Lord's Supper;

○ many more commissions and synods must meet, despite the fact that so many have met already and the results of their meetings have simply been ignored;

○ there must be much more 'prayer', as if all the prayers for unity throughout the ages were insufficient;

○ there must be much more patient 'suffering' in the divided Church, as though the suffering that has been caused to mankind, nations and communities, married couples and families by the division in the Church has not been crying to heaven for long enough already.

One is almost tempted to enlist the help of the exorcism: 'Go out, you unholy spirit!' Go out, you who divide and separate, delay and protract! Go out of your churches and centres, faculties and institutions, authorities and commissions! Go out of the hearts of men and out of our hearts! And make room!

Make room for the *Holy Spirit*, who is both tender and strong, who reconciles and unites and who is the power and might of God himself—the Holy Spirit, who is not a mysterious and magic fluid or an animistic magic being, but God himself, who is effective and seizes hold of us, but cannot be seized; who gives himself to us, but is not at our disposal; who creates life, but also directs us.

That Spirit of God is not an anonymous power. He has had a name since the one who was abandoned by men and God himself died and was, according to the faith of his own, taken up from death into God's eternal life. Or, as we read in the ancient profession of faith included in Paul's letter to the Romans: 'designated Son of God in power according to the Spirit of holiness by his resurrection from the dead, Jesus Christ our Lord' (Rom 1:4). He is the Spirit of Jesus Christ and his unmistakable sign is freedom: 'Where the Spirit of the Lord is, there is freedom' (2 Cor 3:17). What a gift! What grace!

○ *Veni, sancte Spiritus*—those are the opening words of the sequence of Pentecost, written at a time when Christianity was still undivided. The Holy Spirit cannot be compelled to come—we can only entreat him. We can ask him:

○ *Lava quod est sordidum*—wash what is stained! Expose the self-satisfaction of the churches and cleanse us of our guilt;

○ *Sana quod est saucium*—heal what is wounded! Help those who have been hurt by an unjust Church law and those who have not been treated fairly in the Church—especially women;

○ *Riga quod est aridum*—water what is barren!

Enliven those who have become resigned in the Church and those who have been marginalised and especially let young people live in renewed hope;

○ *Flecte quod est rigidum*—bend what has become rigid! Humiliate the obstinacy of theologians and hierarchies and shake all false security, so that everything will not always remain as it was;

○ *Fove quod est frigidum*—warm what has become cold! Drive out all our fears and anxieties, our prejudices and restrictions and open our hearts with your love that knows no bounds;

○ *Rege quod est devium*—direct what is going astray! Enable us to call what is error and unjustice by its name and to work in the Church and in society for truth, justice and peace.

My wish for all of us is that we may be able to live trusting in the activity of the Holy Spirit and drawing from that trust strength: strength to live—an excess of strength to live!—strength to resist and strength to commit ourselves.

Let us try, then, in Christian freedom and Christian frankness, and trusting in the power of the Spirit that creates unity, to use our liberty for the Church of Christ. May the peace of Christ be with us!